Self-Assess Your P-12 Practice or Program Using the NAGC

Newly updated and aligned with NAGC's updated standards, *Self-Assess Your P-12 Practice or Program Using the NAGC Gifted Programming Standards* is designed for teachers and gifted education coordinators to reflect on and improve their teaching practices and gifted education programs. The updated NAGC standards reflect developments in the field since the 2010 version of the standards were published and continue to include only evidence-based practices that support the corresponding student outcomes.

Within this self-study guide, educators will find a practical framework to review, analyze, and improve their gifted education program to align with best practices. The guide provides a step-by-step process that includes review of the student outcomes and evidence based practices for each programming standard, data gathering, completion of a checklist to evaluate practice and prioritize areas needing attention, gap analysis, action planning, and progress check-in. The guide also includes samples for each tool provided, additional resources, questions for further discussion, and examples of sources from which to gather evidence to measure student outcomes.

NAGC is grateful to Susan Corwith, Debbie Dailey, Keri Guilbault, Susan Johnsen, and Diane Pratt for their work as members of the team that developed this self-study guide, and all those who reviewed the materials contained herein. Special thanks go to Chin-Wen Lee and Alicia Cotabish for their leadership in chairing the team. Together they have built a guide for improving practice that will maximize the learning outcomes for our gifted and talented learners.

[signature]

Jonathan Plucker, PhD
President

[signature]

John Segota, MPS, CAE
Executive Director

T0133139

Introduction

Gifted and talented education provides programming and services for students performing at advanced levels and for those with the potential to do so that include identification processes as well as the delivery of differentiated curriculum and instruction. The models found in elementary schools vary from in-class differentiation to full-time pull-out classes and outside-of-school enrichment opportunities; programming options in the secondary grades range from homogeneously grouped classes to Advanced Placement course offerings (Callahan, Moon, & Oh, 2017). The 2019 *Pre-K–Grade 12 Gifted Programming Standards* (PK–12 Standards; Professional Standards Committee, 2019) provide a structure for defining important benchmarks for student outcomes and for using evidence-based practices that are the most effective for students with gifts and talents. The standards are often used as a basis for policies, rules, and procedures that are essential for providing systematic programming and services. While the standards may be addressed and implemented in a variety of ways, they provide important direction and focus to the endeavor of program development. They also help define the comprehensiveness necessary in designing and developing options for students with gifts and talents at the local level. Because the PK–12 Standards are grounded in theory, research, and practice paradigms, they provide an important base for all educational efforts on behalf of gifted learners at all stages of development.

Self-Assess Your P-12 Practice or Program Using the NAGC Gifted Programming Standards, developed by a workgroup from the NAGC Professional Standards Committee, provides a self-study checklist and supporting materials based on the PK–12 Standards to assist gifted program administrators and teachers of students with gifts and talents in assessing programmatic and professional learning needs to realize effective classroom practice and programming for these students. Teachers and program administrators will assess the degree to which they engage in evidence-based practices that positively affect student outcomes.

The self-study guide is intended for two primary audiences: (a) the gifted education teacher, whose focus is on student outcomes, and (b) the gifted program administrator, whose responsibilities include not only addressing student outcomes throughout the school/district but also on providing resources and support to teachers so that they can implement best practices in gifted education.

Why Engage in Self-Study?

Self-study involves systematically investigating one's own practice. Grounded in critical theory and concerned with addressing challenging issues (Berry, 1998; Giroux, 1997; McLaren, 1997), self-study is similar to action research in that systematic processes are employed to identify and explore problems in authentic educational contexts (Hong & Lawrence, 2011). Self-study is undertaken not only by administrators, but also by practitioners who have an administrative focus at the program level. The practice is commonly seen in professional learning activities, strategic planning, and a programmatic accreditation process (see also Attard, 2017; Garin & Harper, 2016; Rincones-Gómez, Hoffman, & Rodríguez-Campos, 2016). The self-study approach has become salient in planning, developing, and implementing educational programs and interventions (see also Dombek, Foorman, Garcia, & Smith, 2016; Phillips, Mazzeo, & Smith, 2016; Smith, Dombek, Foorman, Hook, Lee, Cote, Sanabria, & Stafford, 2016a, 2016b; Smith & Foorman, 2015). The adoption of the self-study approach in the field of education merits our continuous use of this self-study tool as a means for K-12 gifted practitioners and administrators to generate knowledge to inform and improve their practices and programming for advanced learners. The self-study process found within this document will also assist in:

- Planning programs in the early stages of development

- Conducting an internal analysis

- Documenting the need for the program

- Justifying programming approach

- Identifying program strengths and weaknesses

- Determining new directions or components

- Evaluating the program's alignment with state and national standards

By examining one's role in teaching and learning and the factors that impact practice, gifted education personnel can increase their awareness of program strengths and weaknesses. Through a reflective process that includes an examination of supportive evidence, program personnel may have a better understanding of practices, student outcomes, and barriers that may impede services to students with gifts and talents, including those from underrepresented groups, as well as gain greater insight into students' perspectives as learners.

The Self-Study Process

There are six steps in this self-assessment (Figure 1). After completing them, you will be confident in your strengths and have a plan in place to address the areas in your classroom practice or program that need adjustment or additional data to better serve your advanced learners.

Figure 1: Self-Study Process

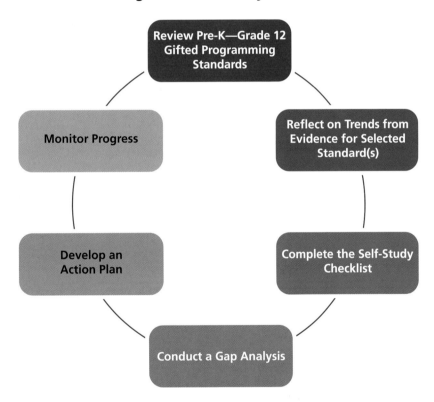

The Self-Study Checklist (Step 3) is designed to be easy to use and can provide a quick visual indication of priorities and needs when planning for high-ability students. Included are tools and examples to assist in documenting progress toward meeting desired student outcomes, as well as a sample template for creating an Action Plan. The Guide also contains resources and suggested questions to help facilitate important conversations with gifted program directors and building and district administrators, as well as the complete set of PK–12 Standards.

1. Review Pre-K–Grade 12 Gifted Programming Standards

The self-study begins with a review of the 2019 Pre-K–Grade 12 Gifted Programming Standards, which can be found in Appendix D. There are six programming standards:

> Standard 1: Learning and Development
>
> Standard 2: Assessment
>
> Standard 3: Curriculum Planning and Instruction
>
> Standard 4: Learning Environments
>
> Standard 5: Programming
>
> Standard 6: Professional Learning

Johnsen, Cotabish, and Dailey (in press) provide a detailed overview and a description of each of the six PK–12 standards. A total of 35 student outcomes and specific evidence-based practices associated with the student outcomes within the six standard areas are also enumerated. These student outcomes and corresponding evidence-based practices provide readers with information that will be revisited at various junctures during the self-study process described in this Guide.

2. Identify Data Sources to Measure Selected Student Outcomes

Following the review of the six standards, begin to identify available data to measure student outcomes, practice, and professional learning information found in the standards. Table 1 provides examples of the types of documents that might provide student outcome information needed to complete the next step, the checklist.

3. Complete the Self-Study Checklist

Informed by previously reviewed data sources, complete the Self-Study Checklist, which consists of four guiding questions posed for each of the student outcomes within a given standard. The four guiding questions are:

1. To what degree do we address this student outcome?

2. To what degree have current practices improved this student outcome?

3. How high of a priority do we place on meeting this standard element?

4. Is support readily available in my district?

Reflect on the availability of sufficient data to inform a response, and if such data exist, then proceed to the response options for each guiding question. Responses range from *"Not at all"* (1) to *"To a great extent"* (4). Checklists for each standard are provided in Appendix A to allow for ease of use, scoring and ranking priorities, and dissemination.

After indicating a response for each of the guiding questions on the Self-Study Checklist, sum points across each row, and then sort the scores calculated in the "Total points" column for each student outcome in increasing value, with items receiving lower point values deemed higher priorities than those with higher scores/lower priorities.

Based on the point values indicated in the column labeled "Total points," rank-order the priorities to be addressed.

4. Conduct a Gap Analysis

After using the Self-Study Checklist to identify the student outcome priorities warranting further attention, the next step is to explore gaps between current and evidence-based practices that improve outcomes for gifted students. A gap analysis requires gathering information, interpreting the trends the information suggests, and determining the additional information and/or changes in practice needed to yield the desired outcomes.

The completion of a gap analysis chart will assist teachers and directors in determining the next steps in ensuring that classroom practice supports the desired student outcomes for gifted and talented students. To use the chart (Table 2):

1. Place the highest priority student outcomes from the Checklist results in Column 1.

2. List the evidence-based practices in Column 2 that corresponds to each outcome. The specific evidence-based practices linked to individual outcomes for each standard are part of the PK–12 Standards document found in Appendix D.

3. After completing Columns 1 and 2, list in Column 3 the current efforts (e.g., classroom practices in which a teacher engages, or strategies a district coordinator employs) that support this practice.

4. Next, indicate in Column 4 the efforts that have occurred in each selected standard area as well as evidence indicating desired student outcomes are being achieved.

   - Don't forget to consider those efforts made in collaboration with general and special education classroom teachers. Although limited evidence might be available at this time, give credit for work that may serve as the foundation for continuous program improvement.

5. In the final column, consider what additional evidence or information is needed to determine if there is a gap between current procedures and practices and those that are based on research. The last two columns identify specific issues or gaps in programming practice(s).

A gap analysis example (see Table 3) that is relevant to both the teacher and coordinator is provided to guide completion of the Gap Analysis

5. Develop an Action Plan

An action plan highlights the steps that must be taken or activities that must be performed well, for a strategy to succeed. The Action Plan Chart (see Table 4) components include:

1. The desired student outcome,

2. Evidence-based practices aligned to a specific P-12 Standard,

3. The identified gap,

4. Supporting and opposing forces that could affect change,

5. Action to close the identified gap,

6. The person(s) responsible for carrying out the action, and

7. A timeline to bring the action to fruition.

Consider the following open-ended questions (e.g., supporting evidence, forces, resources) that impact implementation of change to improve practice and student outcomes under each standard:

- What are two or three actions we could implement to improve student outcomes and teacher practices in each standard?

- What supporting factors promote the implementation of this standard (including those that may exist in general education classrooms)?

- What resisting forces or obstacles hinder the implementation of this standard (including those that may exist in general education classrooms)?

- To what degree will the suggested change in the practice affect current district policy(ies)?

To use the Action Plan Chart:

1. List the desired student outcome in the first column.

2. List the corresponding evidence-based practices in the second column.

3. In Column 3, record the gap identified on the Gap Analysis Chart.

4. Columns 4 and 5 document the supporting and opposing forces that impact services for gifted learners.

   - These may include district or state-level policies, district or state-level funding, personnel or other resources, parental support (or lack of), as well as localized or situational considerations (e.g., community, partnerships, etc.).

5. Column 6 lists the action(s) needed to address the gap and implement the evidence-based practice or need for further information. *Note to program administrators: Remember to include actions that may result from the gifted professional's role as a collaborator with classroom teachers.*

6. The last two columns allow you to designate the person(s) responsible and the time period in which you plan to act.

Teachers of students with gifts and talents and program coordinators will most likely identify program "gaps" and carry out an action plan quite differently due to the nature of their roles in gifted programming. To illustrate this variance in program planning, Table 5 provides examples of action plans based on the roles of the educators. The example of the gifted education teacher is highlighted in gray.

6. Monitor Progress

After finalizing the action plan, periodically, revisit and modify the plan according to environmental changes—new personnel, change in leadership, or new information gained based on research. Additionally, frequent charting of progress towards instituting the evidence-based practices ensures the desired student outcomes are reached. We have created a sample Action Plan Monitoring Tool (see Table 6) to help you assess where you are in the practice and program improvement process.

As you work with this self-study guide, we encourage you to review the resources list in Appendix B to support you in improving gifted and talented student outcomes.

References

Attard, K. (2017). Personally driven professional development: Reflective self-study as a way for teachers to take control of their own professional development. *Teacher Development*, *21*(1), 40–56. https://doi.org/10.1080/13664530.2016.1218363

Berry, K. S. (1998). Nurturing the imagination of resistance: Young adults as creators of knowledge. In J. L. Kincheloe, & S. R. Steinberg (Eds.), *Unauthorized methods: Strategies for critical teaching* (pp. 43–58). Routledge.

Callahan, C. M., Moon, T. R., & Oh, S. (2017). Describing the status of programs for the gifted: A call for action. *Journal for the Education of the Gifted*, *40*(1), 20–49. https://doi.org/10.1177/0162353216686215

Cotabish, A., & Krisel, S. (2012). Action plans: Bringing the program standards to life! In S. K. Johnsen (Ed.), *NAGC Pre-K-Grade 12 gifted education programming standards: A guide to planning and implementing high-quality services* (pp. 231–253). Prufrock Press.

Dombek, J. L., Foorman, B. R., Garcia, M., & Smith, K. G. (2016). *Self-study guide for implementing early literacy interventions* (REL 2016–129). Washington, DC: U.S. Department of Education, Institute of Education Sciences, National Center for Education Evaluation and Regional Assistance, Regional Educational Laboratory Southeast. https://ies.ed.gov/ncee/edlabs/projects/project.asp?projectID=4520

Garin, E., & Harper, M. (2016). A self-study investigation of using inquiry groups in a professional development school context. *School-University Partnerships*, *9*(1), 54–63. https://eric.ed.gov/?id=EJ1107081

Giroux, H. (1997). *Pedagogy and the politics of hope: Theory, culture, and schooling.* Westview.

Hong, C. E., & Lawrence, S. A. (2011). Action research in teacher education: Classroom inquiry, reflection, and data-driven decision making. *Journal of Inquiry & Action in Education*, *4*, 1–17. https://eric.ed.gov/?id=EJ1134554

Johnsen, S. K., Cotabish, A., & Dailey, D. (Eds.) (in press). *NAGC Pre-K-Grade 12 gifted education programming standards: A guide to planning and implementing high-quality services.* Prufrock Press.

McLaren, P. (1997). *Revolutionary multiculturalism: Pedagogies of dissent for the new millennium.* Routledge.

National Association for Gifted Children. (2010). *NAGC Pre-K-Grade 12 gifted programming standards: A blueprint for quality gifted education programs.* Author. https://bit.ly/2010blueprint

Phillips, B. M., Mazzeo, D., & Smith, K. (2016). *Self-study guide for Florida VPK provider improvement plan development.* Washington, DC: U.S. Department of Education, Institute of Education Sciences, National Center for Education Evaluation and Regional Assistance, Regional Educational Laboratory Southeast. https://files.eric.ed.gov/fulltext/ED574650.pdf

Professional Standards Committee. (2019). *2019 Pre-K-Grade 12 gifted programming standards.* National Association for Gifted Children.

Rincones-Gómez, R., Hoffman, L., & Rodríguez-Campos, L. (2016). The model for collaborative evaluations as a framework for the accreditation self-study. *Journal of Emerging Trends in Economics and Management Sciences*, *7*(5), 335–341.

Smith, K. G., Dombek, J. L., Foorman, B. R., Hook, K. S., Lee, L., Cote, A.-M., Sanabria, I., & Stafford, T. (2016a). *Self-study guide for implementing high school academic interventions* (REL 2016–218). Washington, DC: U.S. Department of Education, Institute of Education Sciences, National Center for Education Evaluation and Regional Assistance, Regional Educational Laboratory Southeast. https://ies.ed.gov/ncee/edlabs/projects/project.asp?projectID=4505

Smith, K. G., Dombek, J. L., Foorman, B. R., Hook, K. S., Lee, L., Cote, A.-M., Sanabria, I., & Stafford, T. (2016b). *Self-study guide for implementing literacy interventions in grades 3-8* (REL 2016–224). Washington, DC: U.S. Department of Education, Institute of Education Sciences, National Center for Education Evaluation and Regional Assistance, Regional Educational Laboratory Southeast. https://ies.ed.gov/ncee/edlabs/projects/project.asp?projectID=4543

Smith, K. G., & Foorman, B. R. (2015). *Summer reading camp self-study guide* (REL 2015–070). Washington, DC: U.S. Department of Education, Institute of Education Sciences, National Center for Education Evaluation and Regional Assistance, Regional Educational Laboratory Southeast. https://ies.ed.gov/ncee/edlabs/projects/project.asp?projectID=463

Table 1: Examples of Evidence Sources that Address Student Outcomes

P-12 Standard	Teachers of Students with Gifts and Talents	Program Administrators
Learning and Development	Observations; student journals; Socratic seminars; student self-reflections; learner profiles and portfolios; dynamic learning activities; interviews with family	Curriculum in place to address affective growth; student surveys; records of out-of-school resources used; parent conferences; learning inventories; district program design for all levels; counselor-led professional learning modules
Assessment	Formative and summative assessments; ability and achievement data; assessments related to interests and talent domain; local student assessments; learner profiles and portfolios; retention in gifted education services; above-grade-level testing and/or talent search data	Reviewed and updated district assessment procedure; formative and summative assessments; referrals for gifted services by school; demographic data for gifted education vs. school district; data of annual progress measurement; retention in gifted education services by school; Talent Search participation; differentiated assessment tools; professional learning for classroom teachers on classroom indicators of giftedness and program identification; website with identification information
Curriculum Planning and Instruction	Formative and ongoing assessments; documented student growth (knowledge and skills) commensurate with aptitude; talent development in student's area of interest and/or multiple talent areas across the dimension of learning; high articulation of and engagement with advanced curriculum	Curriculum maps/scope and sequence; differentiated lesson plans; district acceleration plan; use of Depth of Knowledge; observations; evaluator walk-throughs; program evaluation results; collaboration between gifted education specialists and classroom teachers on differentiated instructional practices that meet the needs of gifted students; gifted education specialists share resources that will assist with differentiated learning for general classrooms; strength-based Response to Intervention (RtI) support provided by the gifted education professional; professional learning on culturally responsive curriculum
Learning Environments	Dispositions toward academic and creative productivity; positive peer relationships and social interactions; responsible behavior and leadership; collaboration with diverse individuals and across diverse groups; employment of strategies to address social justice issues; advanced oral and written communication skills and creative expression	Student surveys; student and teacher classroom observations; examples of using formative feedback; classroom groupings; before/after school groups/clubs; leadership projects; evidence of collaboration with classroom and English language learners (ELL) teachers; Socratic seminars with students; results of program evaluation; guest lectures on underrepresented groups in gifted education and related diversity issues
Programming	Parent-teacher conferences; anecdotes; meeting logs with classroom teachers; vertical articulation of program; curriculum maps; district policy guides; career curriculum; collaboration between gifted education specialists and classroom teachers that results in accommodating gifted learners in the regular classroom setting (RtI, differentiation, MTSS, etc.); conversations/feedback/indicators from students, counselors, classroom teachers, parents that indicate the level of social/emotional/behavioral health of the student	Parent conferences; district gifted education budget; district programming scope and sequence; district policies; acceleration addressed along with identification and programming procedures; identification procedures match the definition of giftedness used by the school/district; participation in Advanced Placement, International Baccalaureate, postsecondary enrollment options, etc.; professional learning opportunities; collaboration with special and general education teachers that allows gifted students to continue pursuit of learning that originates in the gifted classroom; participation of gifted education professionals on district/building RtI teams; program design and implementation responsibility assigned to trained personnel; consistency between state definition and program guidelines; description of roles of key gifted education personnel; established schedule for gathering RtI or Multi-Tiered System of Support (MTSS) data (e.g., program evaluation plan) and information about school/district-level decision-making
Professional Learning	Gifted education endorsement or certification; peer coaching; department meetings; meetings with classroom teachers; webinars; online classes; conference attendance; conference presentations; advanced degrees; participation in professional learning communities	Evidence of an annual professional learning plan; participation in conferences/webinars/classes; attainment of gifted education endorsement or certification; degree in gifted education; participation in professional learning communities; gifted education leadership roles within the district/region/state/nation; professional learning linked to gifted education teacher's identification of areas for personal growth

Table 2: Gap Analysis Chart

1	2	3	4	5
Standard/Desired student outcome	Evidence-based practices	What do we do to support this practice?	What evidence do we have that current practices are leading to the desired student outcome?	Gaps: What additional information or change in practice is needed?

Table 3: Example of Gap Analysis *(Teacher example is highlighted in gray.)*

Standard/Desired student outcome	Evidence-based practices	What do we do to support this practice?	What evidence do we have that current practices are leading to the desired student outcome?	Gaps: What additional information or change in practice is needed?
5.1. Students with gifts and talents demonstrate growth commensurate with their abilities in cognitive, social-emotional, and psychosocial areas as a result of comprehensive programming and services.	5.1.1. Educators use multiple approaches to accelerate learning within and outside of the school setting.	Assign enrichment activities found in the teacher's edition textbook. Not sure what other alternative approaches can be used to accelerate learning.	No evidence related to 5.1.1.	Search for evidence-based approaches to accelerate learning and compare against current classroom practice. Understand how to increase collaboration between the coordinator and classroom teachers that results in accommodating gifted learners in the general education classroom setting. Curriculum mapping and vertical articulation of the program are also needed.
2.1. All students in Pre-K through grade 12 with gifts and talents have equal access to the identification process and proportionally represent each campus.	2.1.1. Educators develop environments and instructional activities that prepare and encourage students from diverse backgrounds to express characteristics and behaviors that are associated with giftedness.	We currently collect learner profiles and portfolios, formative and summative assessment measures, student program evaluations, demographic data, ability and achievement data, data analysis, local student assessments. We do not use this information to differentiate types of activities.	We have evidence of students' progress but have no mechanism in place to assess for giftedness.	Teachers need to understand the characteristics of giftedness to guide classroom activities. Need a tool to assess.

Table 4: Action Plan

Standard/ Desired student outcome	Evidence-based practices	Identified gaps	Supporting forces	Opposing forces	Action(s) to address the identified gap (Practice or Research)	Person(s) responsible	Timeline

Adapted with permission from National Association for Gifted Children. (2010). *NAGC Pre-K-Grade 12 gifted programming standards: A blueprint for quality gifted education programs.* Author. https://bit.ly/2010blueprint

Table 5: Action Plan Example *(Teacher example is highlighted in gray.)*

Standard/ Desired student outcome	Evidence-based practices	Identified gaps	Supporting forces	Opposing forces	Action(s) to address the identified gap (Practice or Research)	Person(s) responsible	Timeline
5.1. Students with gifts and talents demonstrate growth commensurate with their abilities in cognitive, social-emotional, and psychosocial areas as a result of comprehensive programming and services.	5.1.1. Educators use multiple approaches to accelerate learning within and outside of the school setting.	Additional evidence of acceleration is needed. Search for evidence-based approaches to accelerate learning and compare against current practice.	Program Coordinator; administration	Additional programming options may not be viable options due to limited district funds.	Collect additional evidence of accelerative practices for comparative purposes; Ask Program Coordinator to provide professional learning activities to school personnel.	Teacher(s) of the gifted; Program Coordinator	One semester
2.1. All students in Pre-K through grade 12 with gifts and talents have equal access to the identification process and proportionally represent each campus.	2.1.1. Educators develop environments and instructional activities that prepare and encourage students from diverse backgrounds to express characteristics and behaviors that are associated with giftedness.	Teachers need to understand the characteristics of giftedness to guide classroom instruction and activities.	Building principal makes identifying students from diverse populations a priority.	State requires professional learning activities to be linked to the state's educational priorities.	Provide school-wide professional learning activities to increase understanding about the characteristics of giftedness. Tie to state educational priorities.	Program Coordinator	One month

Adapted with permission from Cotabish, A., & Krisel, S. (2012). Action plans: Bringing the program standards to life! In S. Johnsen (Ed.), *NAGC Pre-K-Grade 12 gifted education programming standards: A guide to planning and implementing high-quality services* (pp. 231–253). Prufrock Press.

Table 6: Action Plan Monitoring Tool

Standard/ Desired student outcome	Evidence-based practices	Identified gaps	Action(s) to address the identified gap (Practice or Research)	Person(s) responsible	Progress to date

APPENDIX A

Self-Study Checklist

Directions: Place a checkmark in the box that corresponds to the degree that each student outcome in each of the six programming standards is addressed. Place a checkmark in Column 4b if the component warrants further discussion with the program coordinator or other school administrator. Calculate the number of points in each row and list under the "Total Points" column. After completing each section, rank-order the "Total Points" column. Use the ranking to inform teaching and program priorities related to each standard (lower points indicate a higher priority).

Self-Study Checklist Example

The following is an example of a completed Standard 3 checklist. The total of ratings (points) was calculated across each row of student outcomes and placed in the "Total Points" column. After calculating the sum total, the "Total Points" column was used to inform the rank order of student outcome priorities that need to be addressed in the gifted program. Lower total points values indicate higher program priorities. Please note that the rank order component of this checklist is simply a guide to assist you in the decision-making process as you contemplate instructional and program priorities.

Completed Standard 3 Self-Study Checklist Example

Programming Standard 3: Curriculum Planning and Instruction	Question 1 — To what degree do we address the student outcome?				Question 2 — To what degree have current practices improved this student outcome?				Question 3 — How high of a priority do we place on meeting this standard element?				Question 4a — Is support readily available in my district? (check 4b to indicate a need to address with the coordinator or other administrator)				Question 4b	Total points	Rank order of priorities to address
	Not at all 1	2	3	To a great extent 4	Not at all 1	2	3	To a great extent 4	Low 1	2	3	High 4	Not at all 1	2	3	To a great extent 4			
Student Outcomes																			
3.1. *Curriculum Planning.* Students with gifts and talents demonstrate academic growth commensurate with their abilities each school year.			✓			✓					✓				✓		☑	11	
3.2. *Talent Development.* Students with gifts and talents demonstrate growth in social and emotional and psychosocial skills necessary for achievement in their domain(s) of talent and/or areas of interest.		✓				✓						✓		✓			✓	10	
3.3. *Responsiveness to Diversity.* Students with gifts and talents develop knowledge and skills for living in and contributing to a diverse and global society.				✓		✓						✓		✓			✓	12	
3.4. *Instructional Strategies.* Students with gifts and talents demonstrate their potential or level of achievement in their domain(s) of talent and/or areas of interest.			✓				✓				✓					✓	✓	13	
3.5. *Instructional Strategies.* Students with gifts and talents become independent investigators.				✓				✓			✓					✓	✓	15	
3.6. *Resources.* Students with gifts and talents are able to demonstrate growth commensurate with their abilities as a result of access to high-quality curricular resources.			✓				✓			✓					✓		✓	11	

Self-Study Checklist Programming Standard 1

Programming Standard 1: Learning and Development	Question 1 — To what degree do we address the student outcome?				Question 2 — To what degree have current practices improved this student outcome?				Question 3 — How high of a priority do we place on meeting this standard element?				Question 4a — Is support readily available in my district? (check 4b to indicate a need to address with the coordinator or other administrator)				Question 4b	Total points	Rank order of priorities to address
	Not at all 1	2	3	To a great extent 4	Not at all 1	2	3	To a great extent 4	Low 1	2	3	High 4	Not at all 1	2	3	To a great extent 4	☑		

Student Outcomes

1.1. Self-Understanding. Students with gifts and talents recognize their interests, strengths, and needs in cognitive, creative, social, emotional, and psychological areas.

1.2. Self-Understanding. Students with gifts and talents demonstrate understanding of how they learn and recognize the influences of their identities, cultures, beliefs, traditions, and values on their learning and behavior.

1.3. Self-Understanding. Students with gifts and talents demonstrate understanding of and respect for similarities and differences between themselves and their cognitive and chronological peer groups and others in the general population.

1.4. Awareness of Needs. Students identify and access supplemental, outside-of-school resources that support the development of their gifts and talents (e.g., families, mentors, experts, or programs).

1.5. Cognitive, Psychosocial, and Affective Growth. Students with gifts and talents demonstrate cognitive growth and psychosocial skills that support their talent development as a result of meaningful and challenging learning activities that address their unique characteristics and needs.

1.6. Cognitive Growth and Career Development. Students with gifts and talents identify future career goals that match their interests and strengths. Students determine resources needed to meet those goals (e.g., supplemental educational opportunities, mentors, financial support).

National Association for Gifted Children

Self-Study Checklist Programming Standard 2

Programming Standard 2: Assessment	Question 1 — To what degree do we address the student outcome?				Question 2 — To what degree have current practices improved this student outcome?				Question 3 — How high of a priority do we place on meeting this standard element?				Question 4a — Is support readily available in my district? (check 4b to indicate a need to address with the coordinator or other administrator)				Question 4b	Total points	Rank order of priorities to address
	Not at all 1	2	3	To a great extent 4	Not at all 1	2	3	To a great extent 4	Low 1	2	3	High 4	Not at all 1	2	3	To a great extent 4			
Student Outcomes																			
2.1. *Identification.* All students in Pre-K through grade 12 with gifts and talents have equal access to the identification process and proportionally represent each campus.																			
2.2. *Identification.* Students with gifts and talents are identified for services that match their interests, strengths, and needs.																	☑		
2.3. *Identification.* Students with identified gifts and talents represent diverse backgrounds.																			
2.4. *Learning Progress.* As a result of using multiple and ongoing assessments, students with gifts and talents demonstrate growth commensurate with abilities in cognitive, social-emotional, and psychosocial areas.																			
2.5. *Learning Progress.* Students self-assess their learning progress.																			

Self-Study Checklist Programming Standard 3

Programming Standard 3: Curriculum Planning and Instruction	Question 1 — To what degree do we address the student outcome?				Question 2 — To what degree have current practices improved this student outcome?				Question 3 — How high of a priority do we place on meeting this standard element?				Question 4a — Is support readily available in my district? (check 4b to indicate a need to address with the coordinator or other administrator)				Question 4b	Total points	Rank order of priorities to address
	Not at all 1	2	3	To a great extent 4	Not at all 1	2	3	To a great extent 4	Low 1	2	3	High 4	Not at all 1	2	3	To a great extent 4			
Student Outcomes																	☑		
3.1. *Curriculum Planning.* Students with gifts and talents demonstrate academic growth commensurate with their abilities each school year.																			
3.2. *Talent Development.* Students with gifts and talents demonstrate growth in social and emotional and psychosocial skills necessary for achievement in their domain(s) of talent and/or areas of interest.																			
3.3. *Responsiveness to Diversity.* Students with gifts and talents develop knowledge and skills for living in and contributing to a diverse and global society.																			
3.4. *Instructional Strategies.* Students with gifts and talents demonstrate their potential or level of achievement in their domain(s) of talent and/or areas of interest.																			
3.5. *Instructional Strategies.* Students with gifts and talents become independent investigators.																			
3.6. *Resources.* Students with gifts and talents are able to demonstrate growth commensurate with their abilities as a result of access to high-quality curricular resources.																			

Self-Study Checklist Programming Standard 4

Programming Standard 4: Learning Environments	Question 1 — To what degree do we address the student outcome?				Question 2 — To what degree have current practices improved this student outcome?				Question 3 — How high of a priority do we place on meeting this standard element?				Question 4a — Is support readily available in my district? (check 4b to indicate a need to address with the coordinator or other administrator)				Question 4b	Total points	Rank order of priorities to address
	Not at all 1	2	3	To a great extent 4	Not at all 1	2	3	To a great extent 4	Low 1	2	3	High 4	Not at all 1	2	3	To a great extent 4	☑		
Student Outcomes																			
4.1. Personal Competence. Students with gifts and talents demonstrate growth in personal competence and dispositions for exceptional academic and creative productivity. These include self-awareness, self-efficacy, confidence, motivation, resilience, independence, curiosity, and risk taking.																			
4.2. Social Competence. Students with gifts and talents develop social competence manifested in positive peer relationships and social interactions.																			
4.3. Responsibility and Leadership. Students with gifts and talents demonstrate personal and social responsibility.																			
4.4. Cultural Competence. Students with gifts and talents value their own and others' language, heritage, and circumstance. They possess skills in communicating, teaming, and collaborating with diverse individuals and across diverse groups. They use positive strategies to address social issues, including discrimination and stereotyping.																			
4.5. Communication Competence. Students with gifts and talents develop competence in interpersonal and technical communication skills. They demonstrate advanced oral and written skills and creative expression. They display fluency with technologies that support effective communication and are competent consumers of media and technology.																			

Self-Study Checklist Programming Standard 5

Programming Standard 5: Programming	Question 1: To what degree do we address the student outcome?				Question 2: To what degree have current practices improved this student outcome?				Question 3: How high of a priority do we place on meeting this standard element?				Question 4a: Is support readily available in my district? (check 4b to indicate a need to address with the coordinator or other administrator)				Question 4b	Total points	Rank order of priorities to address
	Not at all 1	2	3	To a great extent 4	Not at all 1	2	3	To a great extent 4	Low 1	2	3	High 4	Not at all 1	2	3	To a great extent 4	☑		
Student Outcomes																			
5.1. *Comprehensiveness.* Students with gifts and talents demonstrate growth commensurate with their abilities in cognitive, social-emotional, and psychosocial areas as a result of comprehensive programming and services.																			
5.2. *Cohesive and Coordinated Services.* Students with gifts and talents demonstrate yearly progress commensurate with ability as a result of a continuum of Pre-K–12 services and coordination between gifted, general, special, and related professional services, including outside of school learning specialists and advocates.																			
5.3. *Career Pathways.* Students with gifts and talents create future career-oriented goals and identify talent development pathways to reach those goals.																			
5.4. *Collaboration.* Students with gifts and talents are able to continuously advance their talent development and achieve their learning goals through regular collaboration among families, community members, advocates, and the school.																			
5.5. *Resources.* Students with gifts and talents participate in gifted education programming that is adequately staffed and funded to meet students' interests, strengths, needs.																			

Programming Standard 5: Programming	Question 1 To what degree do we address the student outcome?				Question 2 To what degree have current practices improved this student outcome?				Question 3 How high of a priority do we place on meeting this standard element?				Question 4a Is support readily available in my district? (check 4b to indicate a need to address with the coordinator or other administrator)				Question 4b	Total points	Rank order of priorities to address
	Not at all			To a great extent	Not at all			To a great extent	Low			High	Not at all			To a great extent	☑		
	1	2	3	4	1	2	3	4	1	2	3	4	1	2	3	4			
Student Outcomes																			
5.6. *Policies and Procedures.* Students with gifts and talents participate in general and gifted education programs guided by clear policies and procedures that provide for their advanced learning needs (e.g., early entrance, acceleration, credit in lieu of enrollment).																			
5.7. *Evaluation of Programming and Services.* Students with gifts and talents demonstrate yearly learning progress commensurate with abilities as a result of high-quality programming and services matched to their interests, strengths, and needs.																			
5.8. *Evaluation of Programming and Services.* Students with gifts and talents have access to programming and services required for the development of their gifts and talents as a result of ongoing evaluation and program improvements.																			

Programming Standard 6: Professional Learning	Question 1 — To what degree do we address the student outcome?				Question 2 — To what degree have current practices improved this student outcome?				Question 3 — How high of a priority do we place on meeting this standard element?				Question 4a — Is support readily available in my district? (check 4b to indicate a need to address with the coordinator or other administrator)				Question 4b	Total points	Rank order of priorities to address
	Not at all 1	2	3	To a great extent 4	Not at all 1	2	3	To a great extent 4	Low 1	2	3	High 4	Not at all 1	2	3	To a great extent 4	☑		
Student Outcomes																			
6.1. Talent Development. Students identify and fully develop their talents and gifts as a result of interacting with educators who possess content pedagogical knowledge and meet national teacher preparation standards in gifted education and the Standards for Professional Learning.																			
6.2. Psychosocial and Social-Emotional Development. Students with gifts and talents develop critical psychosocial skills and show social-emotional growth as a result of educators and counselors who have participated in professional learning aligned with national standards in gifted education and Standards for Professional Learning.																			
6.3. Equity and Inclusion. All students with gifts and talents are able to develop their abilities as a result of educators who are committed to removing barriers to access and creating inclusive gifted education communities.																			
6.4. Lifelong Learning. Students develop their gifts and talents as a result of educators who are lifelong learners, participating in ongoing professional learning and continuing education opportunities.																			
6.5. Ethics. All students with gifts and talents, including those who may be twice exceptional, English language learners, or who come from underrepresented populations receive equal opportunities to be identified and served in high-quality gifted programming as a result of educators who are guided by ethical practices.																			

APPENDIX B

Additional Resources

There is useful information on the NAGC website that we recommend you review to increase your familiarity with gifted and talented education or to recommend to others.

Terminology Used in Gifted Education

To speak the language of gifted education, it is important to familiarize yourself with the commonly used terms. While used frequently in professional literature and documents as well as professional conversations, gifted education administrators and teachers should avoid using them without explanation in meetings with parents and non-school personnel. Review the "Glossary of Terms" (https://bit.ly/nagcglossary) webpage and use them appropriately in professional conversations.

It is also important to familiarize yourself with the terms used in the PK–12 standards. Review the "Programming Standards Glossary of Terms" (https://bit.ly/2019glossary) webpage (see also Appendix E).

Frequently Asked Questions

There are often many questions about gifted and talented education, including the definition of giftedness, who makes decisions about gifted programming, how much money is spent on gifted programming, and how much training does a teacher need to work with gifted students. Review the "Frequently Asked Questions about Gifted Education" (https://bit.ly/nagcfaq) webpage.

Myths About Students With Gifts and Talents

There are often many myths about advanced learners. Review the "Myths about Gifted Students" (https://bit.ly/nagcmyths) webpage to gain a better understanding of these frequent misunderstandings.

Tools for Administrators

Many tools and resources have been developed by administrators for administrators to pave the way for districts to offer a challenging and appropriate education for gifted and talented learners, including a list of 10 things all administrators should know about gifted children, links to administrator-focused journal articles about gifted education, and videos on the basic tenets of gifted education and other topics. Review the Administrator Toolbox section on the "Resources for Administrators" (https://bit.ly/nagcadmin) webpage. You may also want to get the questions for administrators from Appendix C into the building- and district-level administrators' hands.

Underrepresented Groups in Gifted Education

Too often, children from minority, ELL, and low-income backgrounds are overlooked for gifted and talented programming. Visit the "Increasing Equity in Gifted Education Programs and Services" (https://bit.ly/nagcequity) webpage for links to key reports and articles that provide topic overviews and strategies to address this pervasive issue.

Addressing Standards: Growth Expectations for Gifted Learners

With the adoption of the Common Core State Standards in Mathematics and Language Arts, and the introduction of the Next Generation Science Standards, gifted education administrators and teachers must understand the progression of growth expected from gifted and talented students. Due to their high test scores and test ceiling effects among this special group, there is often a tendency to ignore advanced learners and their special learning needs. Visit the "Common Core State Standards, National Science Standards and Gifted Education" (https://bit.ly/nagcccss) webpage for multiple resources.

Acceleration

Acceleration is one of the most effective research-based interventions for the academic growth of students who are ready for an advanced or faster-paced curriculum. The overwhelming research evidence in favor of acceleration makes the intervention a highly valued, cost-effective option for all schools. The evidence is compelling that, for highly motivated gifted students, acceleration must be an option; therefore, all schools need to have written policies that allow the possibility of the various forms of acceleration as an academic intervention for carefully selected high-ability students. Visit the "Acceleration" (https://bit.ly/nagcacceleration) webpage for resources, including a link to 2018 Developing Academic Acceleration Policies (https://bit.ly/2018accpolicy).

APPENDIX C
Preparing for Future Conversations

1. Self-Reflection Questions for Teachers of Students with Gifts and Talents

To promote personal reflection and prepare for discussions with the gifted and talented program coordinator about improving student outcomes, teacher practice, and gifted programming, consider the following questions:

1. Identify the three most common challenges you have in implementing the NAGC Pre-K–Grade 12 Gifted Programming Standards. What are the factors underlying the challenges and what are some possible approaches to resolve them?

2. What data have you used to determine students with gifts and talents are achieving the outcomes enumerated in the NAGC Pre-K–Grade 12 Gifted Programming Standards?

3. What data or policies are needed to ensure that key decisions about high-ability students in your building are based on appropriate evidence?

4. What three key points about gifted and talented identification and programming would you share with all professionals in your building (and why)?

5. How do your services strengthen gifted behaviors for underrepresented students who may not be identified through traditional identification approaches?

6. What opportunities do you see that would allow you to provide additional services for students with gifts and talents?

7. How do you collaborate with colleagues in your building to ensure the needs of students with gifts and talents are being appropriately addressed? What opportunities are there to improve collaboration?

8. What opportunities are there to obtain targeted professional learning to address gaps in your evidence-based practice?

2. Self-Reflection Questions for Gifted and Talented Program Coordinators

To promote personal reflection and prepare for discussions with building and district administrators about improving student outcomes, teacher practice, and gifted programming, consider the following questions:

1. Identify the most common challenges teachers have in implementing the NAGC Pre-K–Grade 12 Gifted Programming Standards. What are the factors underlying the challenges and what are some possible approaches to resolve them?

2. What data are available to indicate whether gifted students are achieving the outcomes enumerated in the NAGC Pre-K–Grade 12 Gifted Programming Standards?

3. What data or policies are needed to ensure that key decisions about high-ability students in your building/district are based on appropriate evidence?

4. What three key points about gifted and talented identification and programming would you share with all teachers and other school professionals (and why)?

5. Does the make-up of the gifted program population reflect school district demographics? If not, how will you work with teachers, counselors, parents, students, and administrators to increase the number of underrepresented students in the gifted and talented program?

6. What policies are needed to facilitate a continuum of services for gifted students?

7. How do you work with teachers to build a collaborative working environment to ensure the needs of students with gifts and talents are being appropriately addressed? What strengths and needs do you see in these relationships? What opportunities are there to improve collaboration?

8. What professional learning opportunities do classroom teachers have that will build/develop strategies for working with students with gifts and talents?

3. Information Gathering Questions for Building Administrators Other than the Gifted and Talented Program Coordinators (e.g., principal, professional learning coordinator)

To learn more about the progress of students in the gifted education program, discuss the following questions with the gifted and talented program coordinator in your school:

1. Identify the most common challenges you and the teachers of students with gifts and talents have in implementing the NAGC Pre-K–Grade 12 Gifted Programming Standards. What are the factors underlying the challenges and what are some possible approaches to resolve them?

2. What do the data tell us about whether students with gifts and talents are achieving the outcomes enumerated in the NAGC Pre-K–Grade 12 Gifted Programming Standards?

3. What additional data or policies do we need to ensure that we are making high-quality decisions about whom we identify as gifted and the services they receive?

4. What two or three key points about gifted and talented identification and programming would you want to share with the entire staff? How could I help you do this?

5. How can we work together to increase the number of underrepresented students in the gifted and talented program?

6. Are there changes that could be made to the building schedule that would allow a stronger continuum of services for students with gifts and talents?

7. Are there areas that need attention in building a collaborative work culture in this building to ensure the needs of students with gifts and talents are being appropriately addressed?

8. Are there professional learning areas that need attention in order to effectively implement the standards?

National Association for Gifted Children

APPENDIX D
2019 Pre-K–Grade 12 Gifted Programming Standards

STANDARD 1: LEARNING AND DEVELOPMENT

Description: Educators understand the variations in learning and development in cognitive, affective, and psychosocial areas between and among individuals with gifts and talents, creating learning environments that encourage awareness and understanding of interests, strengths, and needs; cognitive growth, social and emotional, and psychosocial skill development in school, home, and community settings.

STUDENT OUTCOMES	EVIDENCE-BASED PRACTICES
1.1. Self-Understanding. Students with gifts and talents recognize their interests, strengths, and needs in cognitive, creative, social, emotional, and psychological areas.	1.1.1. Educators engage students with gifts and talents in identifying interests, strengths, and needs. 1.1.2. Educators engage students with gifts and talents in identifying their intellectual, academic, creative, leadership, and/or artistic abilities. 1.1.3. Educators engage students in developmentally appropriate activities that help them discover their talents and develop noncognitive skills that support their talent areas.
1.2. Self-Understanding. Students with gifts and talents demonstrate understanding of how they learn and recognize the influences of their identities, cultures, beliefs, traditions, and values on their learning and behavior.	1.2.1. Educators develop activities that match each student's developmental level and culture-based learning needs. 1.2.2. Educators assist students with gifts and talents in developing identities consistent with their potential and areas of talent. 1.2.3. Teachers create a learning environment that promotes high expectations for all children, support for perceived failures, positive feedback, respect for different cultures and values, and addresses stereotypes and biases.
1.3. Self-Understanding. Students with gifts and talents demonstrate understanding of and respect for similarities and differences between themselves and their cognitive and chronological peer groups and others in the general population.	1.3.1. Educators use evidence-based instructional and grouping practices to allow students with similar gifts, talents, abilities, and strengths to learn together, and also create opportunities for students to interact with individuals of various gifts, talents, abilities, strengths, and goals. 1.3.2. Educators model respect for individuals with diverse abilities, interests, strengths, learning needs, and goals. 1.3.3. Educators discuss and explain developmental differences and use materials and instructional activities matched to students' varied abilities, interests, and learning needs.
1.4. Awareness of Needs. Students identify and access supplemental, outside-of-school resources that support the development of their gifts and talents (e.g., families, mentors, experts, or programs).	1.4.1. Educators provide role models for students with gifts and talents that match their interests, strengths, and needs. 1.4.2. Educators identify outside-of-school learning opportunities and community resources that match students' interests, strengths, and needs. 1.4.3. Educators gather information and inform students and families about resources available to develop their child's talents.
1.5. Cognitive, Psychosocial, and Affective Growth. Students with gifts and talents demonstrate cognitive growth and psychosocial skills that support their talent development as a result of meaningful and challenging learning activities that address their unique characteristics and needs.	1.5.1. Educators use evidence-based approaches to grouping and instruction that promote cognitive growth and psychosocial and social-emotional skill development for students with gifts and talents. 1.5.2. Educators design interventions for students that are based on research of effective practices and provide accommodations for learning differences to develop cognitive and noncognitive abilities that support growth and achievement. 1.5.3. Educators develop specialized, research-supported intervention services for students with gifts and talents who are underachieving (whose learning is not commensurate with their abilities) to develop their talents.
1.6. Cognitive Growth and Career Development. Students with gifts and talents identify future career goals that match their interests and strengths. Students determine resources needed to meet those goals (e.g., supplemental educational opportunities, mentors, financial support).	1.6.1. Educators help students identify college and career goals that are consistent with their interests and strengths. 1.6.2. Educators implement learning progressions that incorporate person/social awareness and adjustment, academic planning, psychosocial skill development, and college and career awareness. 1.6.3. Educators provide students with college and career guidance and connect students to college and career resources.

STANDARD 2: ASSESSMENT

Description: Assessments provide information about identification and learning progress for students with gifts and talents.

STUDENT OUTCOMES	EVIDENCE-BASED PRACTICES
2.1. Identification. All students in Pre-K through grade 12 with gifts and talents have equal access to the identification process and proportionally represent each campus.	2.1.1. Educators develop environments and instructional activities that prepare and encourage students from diverse backgrounds to express characteristics and behaviors that are associated with giftedness. 2.1.2. Educators provide parents/guardians with information in their preferred language for communication regarding behaviors and characteristics that are associated with giftedness and with information that explains the nature and purpose of gifted programming options. 2.1.3. Educators use universal screening and multiple indicators of potential and achievement at various grade levels from Pre-K through grade 12 to provide multiple entry points to services designed to meet demonstrated needs.
2.2. Identification. Students with gifts and talents are identified for services that match their interests, strengths, and needs.	2.2.1. Educators establish comprehensive, cohesive, and ongoing policies and procedures for identifying and serving students with gifts and talents. These policies include referral, informed consent, the assessment process, review of all assessment information, student retention, student reassessment, student exiting, and appeals procedures for both entry and exit from gifted programming and services. 2.2.2. Educators select and use assessments that relate to services provided and identify abilities, interests, strengths, and needs based on current research. 2.2.3. Educators use assessments that provide qualitative and quantitative information from a variety of sources. 2.2.4. Educators use assessments that provide information related to above-grade-level performance. 2.2.5. Educators select assessments that minimize bias by including information in the technical manual that describes content in terms of potential bias, includes norms that match national census information or local populations, shows how items discriminate equally well for each group, and provides separate reliability and validity information for each group. 2.2.6. Educators have knowledge of student exceptionalities and collect assessment data while adjusting curriculum and instruction to learn about each student's developmental level and aptitude for learning (i.e., dynamic assessment). 2.2.7. Educators interpret multiple assessments in different domains and understand the uses and limitations of the assessments in identifying the interests, strengths and needs of students with gifts and talents. 2.2.8. Educators inform all parents/guardians about the identification process. Educators obtain parental/guardian permission for assessments, use culturally sensitive checklists, and elicit evidence regarding the child's interests and potential outside of the classroom setting.
2.3. Identification. Students with identified gifts and talents represent diverse backgrounds.	2.3.1. Educators select and use equitable approaches and assessments that minimize bias for referring and identifying students with gifts and talents, attending to segments of the population that are frequently hidden or under identified. Approaches and tools may include front-loading talent development activities, universal screening, using locally developed norms, assuring assessment tools are in the child's preferred language for communication or nonverbal formats, and building relationships with students to understand their unique challenges and needs. 2.3.2. Educators understand and implement district, state, and/or national policies designed to foster equity in gifted programming and services.
2.4. Learning Progress. As a result of using multiple and ongoing assessments, students with gifts and talents demonstrate growth commensurate with abilities in cognitive, social-emotional, and psychosocial areas.	2.4.1. Educators use differentiated formative assessments to develop learning experiences that challenge students with gifts and talents. 2.4.2. Educators use differentiated ongoing product-based and performance-based assessments to measure the academic and social-emotional progress of students with gifts and talents. 2.4.3. Educators use standardized (e.g., adaptive, above-grade-level) and classroom assessments that can measure the academic progress of students with gifts and talents. 2.4.4. Educators use and interpret qualitative and quantitative assessment information to develop a profile of the interests, strengths, and needs of each student with gifts and talents to plan appropriate interventions. 2.4.5. Educators interpret and communicate assessment information to students with gifts and talents and their parents/guardians, and assure information is provided in their preferred language for communication.
2.5. Learning Progress. Students self-assess their learning progress.	2.5.1. Educators provide opportunities for students to set personal goals, keep records, and monitor their own learning progress.

STANDARD 3: CURRICULUM PLANNING AND INSTRUCTION

Description: Educators apply evidence-based models of curriculum and instruction related to students with gifts and talents and respond to their needs by planning, selecting, adapting, and creating curriculum that is responsive to diversity. Educators use a repertoire of instructional strategies to ensure specific student outcomes and measurable growth.

STUDENT OUTCOMES	EVIDENCE-BASED PRACTICES
3.1. Curriculum Planning. Students with gifts and talents demonstrate academic growth commensurate with their abilities each school year.	3.1.1. Educators use local, state, and national content and technology standards to align, expand, enrich, and/or accelerate curriculum and instructional plans. 3.1.2. Educators design a comprehensive and cohesive curriculum and use learning progressions to develop differentiated plans for Pre-K through grade 12 students with gifts and talents. 3.1.3. Educators adapt, modify, or replace the core or standard curriculum to meet the interest, strengths, and needs of students with gifts and talents and those with special needs such as twice exceptional, highly gifted, and English language learners. 3.1.4. Educators design differentiated curriculum that incorporates advanced, conceptually challenging, in-depth, and complex content for students with gifts and talents. 3.1.5. Educators regularly use pre-assessments, formative assessments, and summative assessments to identify students' strengths and needs, develop differentiated content, and adjust instructional plans based on progress monitoring. 3.1.6. Educators pace instruction based on the learning rates of students with gifts and talents and compact, deepen, and accelerate curriculum as appropriate. 3.1.7. Educators integrate a variety of technologies for students to construct knowledge, solve problems, communicate and express themselves creatively, and collaborate with others in teams locally and globally. 3.1.8. Educators consider accommodations and/or assistive technologies to provide equal access to learning opportunities with twice-exceptional learners and other students with developmental differences.
3.2. Talent Development. Students with gifts and talents demonstrate growth in social and emotional and psychosocial skills necessary for achievement in their domain(s) of talent and/or areas of interest.	3.2.1. As they plan curriculum, educators include components that address goal setting, resiliency, self-management, self-advocacy, social awareness, and responsible decision making. 3.2.2. Educators design learning experiences for each stage of talent development to cultivate social and emotional and psychosocial skills that support high achievement and talent development.
3.3. Responsiveness to Diversity. Students with gifts and talents develop knowledge and skills for living in and contributing to a diverse and global society.	3.3.1. Educators develop and use curriculum that is responsive and relevant to diversity that connects to students' real-life experiences and communities and includes multiple voices and perspectives. 3.3.2. Educators encourage students to connect to others' experiences, examine their own perspectives and biases, and develop a critical consciousness. 3.3.3. Educators use high-quality, appropriately challenging materials that include multiple perspectives.
3.4. Instructional Strategies. Students with gifts and talents demonstrate their potential or level of achievement in their domain(s) of talent and/or areas of interest.	3.4.1. Educators select, adapt, and use a repertoire of instructional strategies to differentiate instruction for students with gifts and talents. 3.4.2. Educators provide opportunities for students with gifts and talents to explore, develop, or research in existing domain(s) of talent and/or in new areas of interest. 3.4.3. Educators use models of inquiry to engage students in critical thinking, creative thinking, and problem-solving strategies, particularly in their domain(s) of talent, both to reveal and address the needs of students with gifts and talents.
3.5. Instructional Strategies. Students with gifts and talents become independent investigators.	3.5.1. Educators model and teach metacognitive models to meet the needs of students with gifts and talents such as self-assessment, goal setting, and monitoring of learning. 3.5.2. Educators model and teach cognitive learning strategies such as rehearsal, organization, and elaboration. 3.5.3. Educators scaffold independent research skills within students' domain(s) of talent.
3.6. Resources. Students with gifts and talents are able to demonstrate growth commensurate with their abilities as a result of access to high-quality curricular resources.	3.6.1. Educators use current, evidence-based curricular resources that are effective with students with gifts and talents. 3.6.2. Educators use school and community resources to support differentiation and advanced instruction appropriate to students' interests, strengths, and academic learning needs.

STANDARD 4: LEARNING ENVIRONMENTS

Description: Learning environments foster a love for learning, personal and social responsibility, multicultural competence, and inter-personal and technical communication skills for leadership to ensure specific student outcomes.

STUDENT OUTCOMES	EVIDENCE-BASED PRACTICES
4.1. Personal Competence. Students with gifts and talents demonstrate growth in personal competence and dispositions for exceptional academic and creative productivity. These include self-awareness, self-advocacy, self-efficacy, confidence, motivation, resilience, independence, curiosity, and risk taking.	4.1.1. Educators maintain high expectations for all students with gifts and talents as evidenced in meaningful and challenging activities. 4.1.2. Educators provide opportunities for self-exploration, development and pursuit of interests, and development of identities supportive of achievement (e.g., through mentors and role models) and a love of learning. 4.1.3. Educators create environments that establish trust, support, and collaborative action among diverse students. 4.1.4. Educators provide feedback that promotes perseverance and resilience and focuses on effort, on evidence of potential to meet high standards, and on mistakes as learning opportunities. 4.1.5. Educators provide examples of positive coping skills and opportunities to apply them.
4.2. Social Competence. Students with gifts and talents develop social competence manifested in positive peer relationships and social interactions.	4.2.1. Educators provide learning environments for both solitude and social interaction. 4.2.2. Educators provide opportunities for interaction and learning with intellectual and artistic/creative peers as well as with chronological-age peers. 4.2.3. Educators assess and provide instruction on psychosocial and social and emotional skills needed for success in school, their community, and society.
4.3. Responsibility and Leadership. Students with gifts and talents demonstrate personal and social responsibility.	4.3.1. Educators establish a safe and welcoming climate for addressing personal and social issues and give students a voice in shaping their learning environment. 4.3.2. Educators provide environments for developing many forms of leadership and leadership skills. 4.3.3. Educators provide opportunities to promote lifelong personal and social responsibility through advocacy and real world problem-solving, both within and outside of the school setting.
4.4. Cultural Competence. Students with gifts and talents value their own and others' language, heritage, and circumstance. They possess skills in communicating, teaming, and collaborating with diverse individuals and across diverse groups. They use positive strategies to address social issues, including discrimination and stereotyping.	4.4.1. Educators model appreciation for and sensitivity to students' diverse backgrounds and languages. 4.4.2. Educators model appropriate language and strategies to effectively address issues such as stereotyping, bias, and discriminatory language and behaviors. 4.4.3. Educators provide structured opportunities to collaborate with diverse peers on a common goal.
4.5. Communication Competence. Students with gifts and talents develop competence in interpersonal and technical communication skills. They demonstrate advanced oral and written skills and creative expression. They display fluency with technologies that support effective communication and are competent consumers of media and technology.	4.5.1. Educators provide opportunities for advanced development and maintenance of first and second language(s). 4.5.2. Educators provide resources that reflect the diversity of their student population to enhance oral, written, and artistic forms of communication. 4.5.3. Educators ensure access to advanced communication tools, including assistive technologies, and use of these tools for expressing higher-level thinking and creative productivity. 4.5.4. Educators provide an environment where students use technology to communicate responsibly and express themselves creatively using the platforms, tools, styles, formats, and digital media appropriate to their goals.

STANDARD 5: PROGRAMMING

Description: Educators use evidence-based practices to promote (a) the cognitive, social-emotional, and psychosocial skill development of students with gifts and talents and (b) programming that meets their interests, strengths, and needs. Educators make use of expertise systematically and collaboratively to develop, implement, manage, and evaluate services for students with a variety of gifts and talents to ensure specific student outcomes.

STUDENT OUTCOMES	EVIDENCE-BASED PRACTICES
5.1. Comprehensiveness. Students with gifts and talents demonstrate growth commensurate with their abilities in cognitive, social-emotional, and psychosocial areas as a result of comprehensive programming and services.	5.1.1. Educators use multiple approaches to accelerate learning within and outside of the school setting. 5.1.2. Educators use enrichment options to extend and deepen learning opportunities within and outside of the school setting. 5.1.3. Educators use multiple forms of evidence-based grouping, including clusters, resource rooms, special classes, or special schools. 5.1.4. Educators use individualized learning options such as mentorships, internships, online courses, and independent study. 5.1.5. Educators leverage technology to increase access to high-level programming by providing digital learning options and assistive technologies.
5.2. Cohesive and Coordinated Services. Students with gifts and talents demonstrate yearly progress commensurate with ability as a result of a continuum of Pre-K-12 services and coordination between gifted, general, special, and related professional services, including outside of school learning specialists and advocates.	5.2.1. Educators who provide gifted, general, special, and related professional services collaboratively plan, develop, implement, manage, and evaluate programming and services for students with gifts and talents. 5.2.2. Educators develop a Pre-K through grade 12 continuum of programming and services in relevant student talent areas that is responsive to students' different levels of need for intervention. 5.2.3. Educators plan coordinated learning activities within and across a specific grade level, content area, course, class, and/or programming option.
5.3. Career Pathways. Students with gifts and talents create future career-oriented goals and identify talent development pathways to reach those goals.	5.3.1. Educators provide professional guidance and counseling for individual students regarding their interests, strengths, challenges, needs, and values. 5.3.2. Educators facilitate programming options involving mentorships, internships, and career and technology education programming and match these experiences to student interests, strengths, needs, and goals.
5.4. Collaboration. Students with gifts and talents are able to continuously advance their talent development and achieve their learning goals through regular collaboration among families, community members, advocates, and the school.	5.4.1. Educators regularly engage students, other educators, families, advocates, and community members in collaboration to plan, advocate for, implement, and evaluate systematic, comprehensive, and ongoing services.
5.5. Resources. Students with gifts and talents participate in gifted education programming that is adequately staffed and funded to meet students' interests, strengths, and needs.	5.5.1. Administrators demonstrate support for gifted programming and services through equitable allocation of resources and demonstrated willingness to ensure that students with gifts and talents receive consistent educational services aligned to their interests, strengths, and needs. 5.5.2. Administrators track expenditures at the school level to verify appropriate and sufficient funding for staffing, curriculum and materials, gifted programming, and services. 5.5.3. Administrators hire a diverse pool of educators with knowledge and professional learning in gifted education and the issues affecting students with gifts and talents.
5.6. Policies and Procedures. Students with gifts and talents participate in general and gifted education programs guided by clear policies and procedures that provide for their advanced learning needs (e.g., early entrance, acceleration, credit in lieu of enrollment).	5.6.1. School policy-makers create and approve evidence-based policies and procedures to guide and sustain all components of the program, including assessment, identification, acceleration, and grouping practices. 5.6.2. Educators align programming and services with local, state, or national laws, rules, regulations, and standards.
5.7. Evaluation of Programming and Services. Students with gifts and talents demonstrate yearly learning progress commensurate with abilities as a result of high-quality programming and services matched to their interests, strengths, and needs.	5.7.1. Educators assess the quantity and quality of programming and services provided for students with gifts and talents by disaggregating assessment and yearly progress data and making the results public. 5.7.2. Educators ensure that the assessments used in program evaluation are reliable and valid for the purposes for which they are being used.
5.8. Evaluation of Programming and Services. Students with gifts and talents have access to programming and services required for the development of their gifts and talents as a result of ongoing evaluation and program improvements.	5.8.1. Administrators provide the necessary time and resources to implement an annual evaluation plan developed by persons with expertise in program evaluation and gifted education. 5.8.2. Educators create and implement evaluation plans that are purposeful and evaluate how student-level outcomes are influenced by fidelity of implementation in the following components of gifted education programming: (a) identification, (b) curriculum, (c) instructional programming and services, (d) ongoing assessment of student learning, (e) counseling and guidance programs, (f) teacher qualifications and professional learning, (g) parent/guardian and community involvement, (h) programming resources, (i) programming design, management, and delivery, and (j) school equity efforts for underrepresented students. 5.8.3. Educators disseminate the results of the evaluation, orally and in written form, and explain how they will use the results.

STANDARD 6: PROFESSIONAL LEARNING

Description: All educators (administrators, teachers, counselors, and other instructional support staff) build their knowledge and skills using the NAGC-CEC Teacher Preparation Standards in Gifted and Talented Education, (NAGC-CEC) Advanced Standards in Gifted Education Teacher Preparation, and the Standards for Professional Learning. Institutions of higher education utilize these standards and the NAGC Faculty Standards to ensure quality professional learning experiences in pre-service, initial, and advanced educator preparation programs. Educators frequently assess their professional learning needs related to the standards, develop and monitor their professional learning plans, systematically engage in coaching and learning to meet their identified needs, and align outcomes with educator performance and student curriculum standards. Administrators assure educators have access to sustained, intensive collaborative, job-embedded, and data-driven learning and assure adequate resources to provide for release time, fund continuing education, and offer substitute support. The effectiveness of professional learning is assessed through relevant student outcomes.

STUDENT OUTCOMES	EVIDENCE-BASED PRACTICES
6.1. Talent Development. Students identify and fully develop their talents and gifts as a result of interacting with educators who possess content pedagogical knowledge and meet national teacher preparation standards in gifted education and the Standards for Professional Learning.	6.1.1. State agencies, institutions of higher education, schools and districts provide comprehensive, research-supported professional learning programs for all educators involved in gifted programming and services. This professional learning addresses the foundations of gifted education, characteristics of diverse students with gifts and talents, identification, assessment, curriculum planning and instruction, learning environments, and programming. High-quality professional learning is delivered by those with expertise in gifted education as guided by the NAGC-CEC Teacher Preparation Standards in Gifted and Talented Education. 6.1.2. State agencies, institutions of higher education, schools, and districts provide sustained professional learning for educators that models how to develop learning environments responsive to diversity and instructional activities that lead to student expression of diverse characteristics and behaviors that are associated with giftedness. 6.1.3. State agencies, institutions of higher education, schools, and districts provide educators with professional learning opportunities that address social issues, including anti-intellectualism, equity, and access. 6.1.4. Administrators plan for, budget and provide sufficient human and material resources needed for professional learning in gifted education (e.g., release time, funding for continuing education, substitute support, webinars, and/or mentors). Administrators access Title I and Title II funds as allowed under the Every Student Succeeds Act (ESSA) to meet this expectation. 6.1.5. Educators use their awareness of local, state and national organizations and publications relevant to gifted education to promote learning for students with gifts and talents and their families.
6.2. Psychosocial and Social-Emotional Development. Students with gifts and talents develop critical psychosocial skills and show social-emotional growth as a result of educators and counselors who have participated in professional learning aligned with national standards in gifted education and Standards for Professional Learning.	6.2.1. Educators participate in ongoing professional learning to understand and apply research to practice with regard to psychosocial skills necessary for the development of gifts and talents and social-emotional development of individuals with gifts and talents.
6.3. Equity and Inclusion. All students with gifts and talents are able to develop their abilities as a result of educators who are committed to removing barriers to access and creating inclusive gifted education communities.	6.3.1. Educators participate in professional learning focused on curriculum and pedagogy that are responsive to diversity for individuals with gifts and talents. 6.3.2. Educators recognize their biases, develop philosophies responsive to diversity, commit themselves to removing barriers, and create inclusive learning environments that meet the educational interests, strengths, and needs of diverse students with gifts and talents. 6.3.3. Educators understand how knowledge, perspectives, and historical and current issues influence professional practice and the education and treatment of individuals with gifts and talents both in school and society.
6.4. Lifelong Learning. Students develop their gifts and talents as a result of educators who are lifelong learners, participating in ongoing professional learning and continuing education opportunities.	6.4.1. Educators regularly reflect on and assess their instructional practices, develop professional learning plans, and improve their practices by participating in continuing education opportunities. 6.4.2. Educators participate in professional learning that is sustained over time, incorporates collaboration and reflection, is goal-aligned and data-driven, is coherent, embedded and transferable, includes regular follow-up, and seeks evidence of positive impact on teacher practice and on increased student learning.
6.5. Ethics. All students with gifts and talents, including those who may be twice exceptional, English language learners, or who come from underrepresented populations receive equal opportunities to be identified and served in high-quality gifted programming as a result of educators who are guided by ethical practices.	6.5.1. Educators use professional ethical principles and specialized program standards to guide their practice. 6.5.2. Educators comply with rules, policies, and standards of ethical practice and advocate for rules, policies, and standards that promote equity and access.

APPENDIX E
Programming Standards Glossary of Terms

Ability/Abilities. Capacity to develop competence in an area of human endeavor; also referred to as 'potential'. Abilities can be developed through appropriate formal and informal education experiences and typically are assessed by measures such as intelligence and aptitude tests.

Above-grade-level. Students with gifts and talents are often performing or are ready to learn content beyond the typical age-based grade level. Identifying readiness to learn beyond a student's grade level can be assessed through performance measures and above-grade-level testing, which is also called off-grade testing, out-of-level testing, above-level testing, and off-level testing. Above-grade-level testing is the practice of administering a test that was designed for and normed on an older population to a younger, advanced/gifted student (Warne, 2012). Widely used in Talent Search programs, it is used to increase the test's ceiling and thus provide an accurate picture of the relative ability level of students whose abilities exceed those that can be measured using on-grade level instruments (Matthews, 2008).

Acceleration. Acceleration encourages students to learn at a rate commensurate with their abilities. It is a strategy of progressing through education at rates faster or ages younger than the norm through grade-based or content-based acceleration. Grade-based acceleration includes options that reduce the number of years spent in school such as grade skipping, telescoping, and early admissions; whereas, content-based acceleration is domain-specific and students receive grade-level instruction within their own class or in an advanced grade at an accelerated pace such as cross-grade grouping, single subject acceleration, and continuous progress. (Assouline, Colangelo, VanTassel-Baska, & Lupkowski-Shoplik, 2015; Colangelo, Assouline, & Gross, 2004; Rogers, 2007, 2015; Worrell, Subotnik, Olszewski-Kubilius, & Dixson, 2019).

Achievement. Accomplishment or performance demonstrating learned knowledge and skills. Achievement typically is assessed using standardized achievement tests, curriculum-based assessments, portfolios, and products.

Aptitude. Ability to learn material at advanced rates and levels of understanding in a specific area (e.g., humanities, mathematics, science). Measured by verbal, quantitative, or nonverbal reasoning tests. (Davis, Rimm, & Siegle, 2011; Reis & Housand, 2008).

Assessment. Process of gathering information or using instruments for a specific purpose, typically to determine an individual's status with respect to a characteristic or behavior. Assessment is a broad term that includes identification, instruction, and evaluation.

Bias. A tendency or prejudice toward or against something or someone. Bias is frequently based on stereotypes involving race, ethnicity, culture, language, age, (dis)abilities, family status/composition, gender identity and expression, sex, sexual orientation, socioeconomic status, religious and spiritual values, geographic location, and country of origin. Bias related to gifted education can result in under-identification of students and unequal access to gifted programming and services (Council for Exceptional Children, 2019; National Association for Gifted Children, n.d.; Plucker, 2018).

Cluster grouping. The intentional placement of a small group of students identified as gifted and talented or high achieving in a heterogeneous classroom with a teacher who has received professional learning in gifted education and will modify the pace, instruction, and curriculum for these students (Brulles & Winebrenner, 2011; Gentry, 1996, 2015, 2016).

Cognitive growth/development. The development of thought, reasoning, and intellect as a result of maturation, experiences, and the environment.

Collaboration. A style of interaction between individuals engaged in shared decision-making as they work toward a common goal. Individuals who collaborate have equally valued personal or professional resources to contribute and they share decision-making authority and accountability for outcomes (e.g., educators responsible for G/T and ELL education together planning instruction for English language learners with gifts and talents) (Council of Chief State School Officers, 2013).

Communication competence. Skills and dispositions to effectively express ideas, thoughts, and needs and to understand those of others through one or more medium and one or more language (Smutny, 2008).

Comprehensiveness. Comprehensive programming and services should include an array of services that match students' interests, strengths, and needs and include a variety of approaches including acceleration (grade-based and/or content-based), enrichment, forms of grouping (cluster grouping, resource rooms, special classes, special schools), individualized learning (independent study, mentorships, online courses, internships), and access to appropriate resources and technology (Johnsen, 2012).

Continuum of services. Gifted programming that addresses students with gifts and talents' needs in all settings and across all grade levels. Continuum of services should include alignment of curriculum, instruction, and activities in a cohesive sequence within grade levels and across specific grades, courses, classes, or programming and services (Johnsen, 2012; NAGC, 2014).

Coordinated services. A shared commitment and continuous collaboration among educators within and across different content areas or concentrations (general education, gifted education, special education, counseling, administration, and others) and families to support learners with gifts and talents (NAGC, 2014).

Creativity. "A product or idea that is novel (or original, unique, or unusual) and useful (or has value, or fits, or is appropriate) within a specific social context" (Plucker, 2017, p. 5).

Creative thinking. Thinking in divergent ways; includes a variety of open-ended thinking processes (e.g., generating novel ideas, elaborating on or modifying a concept, thinking analogically or flexibly). Strategies such as ideation, analogous and lateral thinking, visualization, problem-solving promote creative thinking (Sumners, 2015).

Critical thinking. The evaluative thinking process that requires judgment made through critical examination; components of critical thinking may include discerning purpose, evaluating argument, weighing evidence, appraising data and sources for accuracy or bias, using data to support inferences, examining multiple perspectives, and determining implications and consequences.

Cultural competence. Having awareness of one's own cultural identity and views about differences and the ability to learn about and build on the varying cultural and community norms of others (NEA, n.d.). When individuals (or organizations) are culturally competent, they acknowledge and incorporate at all levels the importance of culture, the assessment of cross-cultural relations, the expansion of cultural knowledge, and the adaptation of services to meet cultural

development needs (Cross, 1988; Cross, Bazron, Dennis, & Jacobs, 1989; Ford, 2013).

Culturally responsive curriculum. The curriculum (a) ensures that all students are interested and engaged; (b) connects to what culturally different students want to learn, (c) presents a balanced, comprehensive, and multidimensional view of the topic, issue or event; (d) presents multiple viewpoints; and addresses stereotypes, distortions, and omissions (Banks, 2008; Ford, 2010).

Culturally responsive teaching. Uses the cultural knowledge, prior experiences, and frames of reference of diverse students to make learning more relevant and effective (Griner & Stewart, 2012). This pedagogy recognizes the importance of including students' cultural references in all aspects of learning (Ladson-Billings, 1994). Teachers who are culturally responsive build on students' personal and cultural strengths and "work proactively and assertively to understand, respect, and meet the needs of students from cultural backgrounds that are different from their own" (Ford & Kea, 2009, p. 1).

Curriculum compacting. An instructional technique that involves three steps: assessing students' academic strengths, eliminating content that students have already mastered, and replacing the work that has been eliminated with more challenging and enriching alternatives, some of which are based on students' interests (Renzulli & Reis, 1998).

Curriculum planning. The process of identifying learning goals, objectives, instructional strategies, activities, materials and resources, assessments, and learning progressions based on the major concepts, processes, and standards of the discipline, and the assessment of student differences related to students' readiness, cultural background, abilities, achievements, and subject matter interest (Hockett, 2009).

Differentiated assessment. Differentiated assessments are used to determine the effectiveness of the differentiated curriculum and instruction and to plan for future differentiated learning activities. Differentiated assessments for students with gifts and talents may include above level tests to measure advanced knowledge and skills, open-ended assessments that focus on problem solving and creativity, portfolios showing student growth over time, and performance and product-based rubrics (Johnsen, 2008b; VanTassel-Baska & Hubbard, 2018; VanTassel-Baska & Zuo, 2011).

Differentiated curricula. Differentiation of the curriculum includes "the use of acceleration and advanced materials; the use of complexity to focus on multiple higher level skills, concepts, and resources simultaneously; the use of depth to focus gifted learning in the form of projects and research and the use of creativity to provide the skills and habits of mind that support innovation" (VanTassel-Baska, 2014, p. 380).

Differentiate instruction. When educators differentiate instruction, they make "adaptations in content, process, product, affect, and learning environment in response to student readiness, interests, and learning profile to ensure appropriate challenge and support for the full range of learners in a classroom" (Tomlinson, 2014, p. 198).

Diversity. Understanding and valuing the range and variety of characteristics and beliefs of individuals who demonstrate a wide range of characteristics. Diversity includes race, ethnicity, culture, language, age, (dis)abilities, family status/composition, gender identity and expression, sexual orientation, socioeconomic status, religious and spiritual values, geographic location, and country of origin (Council for Exceptional Children, 2019).

Educators. Educators include all professionals involved with the education of students with gifts and talents. Educators include but are not limited to central office administrators, principals, general educators, special educators, educators of the gifted, instructional and curriculum specialists, counselors, psychologists, and other support personnel (see National Association for Gifted Children Programming Standard 6: Professional Learning).

Enrichment. "Strategies that supplement or go beyond standard grade-level work, but do not result in advanced placement or potential credit" (Davis, Rimm, & Siegle, 2011, p. 127). Gubbins (2014) identified the following categories of enrichment: enrichment in curricular units that expose students to topics or concepts not included in the standard curriculum, enrichment as an extension to the curriculum, and enrichment as a technique for differentiating the curriculum.

Ethics. Professional special educators are guided by ethical principles, practice standards, and professional policies in ways that respect the diverse characteristics and needs of individuals with exceptionalities and their families (CEC, 2015). These principles include maintaining challenging expectations and a high level of professional competence, practicing collegiality with others, developing relationships with families based on mutual respect, using research to inform practice, protecting and supporting physical and psychological safety of students, not tolerating or engaging in any practice that harms students, practicing within professional standards and policies, upholding laws and regulations, advocating for professional conditions and resources, participating in the improvement of the profession and the growth and dissemination of professional knowledge and skills.

Evaluation of programming. Evaluation of programming systematically examines (a) how the programming components are aligned to standards, (b) the degree to which the components are fully implemented, and (c) if the full implementation of the components is having the desired effects on student outcomes. It includes describing specific goals for the evaluation, determining evaluation questions, identifying sources of information, collecting data, analyzing data, and using the data to make decisions (Callahan, 2015).

Evidence-based. Effective educational strategies supported by evidence and research. As defined in the Every Student Succeeds Act (ESSA), evidence-based means an activity, strategy, or intervention that demonstrates a statistically significant effect on improving student outcomes (Every Student Succeeds Act [ESSA], United States Congress, 2015). ESSA delineates "evidence-based" actions according to four categories reflecting the strength of the evidence. These categories include (a) strong evidence supported by one or more well-designed and well-implemented randomized control experimental studies (Tier 1), (b) moderate evidence supported by one or more well-designed and well-implemented quasi-experimental studies (Tier 2), (c) promising evidence supported by one or more well-designed and well-implemented correlational studies with statistical controls for selection bias (Tier 3), and (d) demonstrates a rationale, which are practices that have a well-defined logic model or theory of action, are informed by research or evaluation, and have some effort underway by a SEA, LEA, or outside research organization to determine their effectiveness (Tier 4). (U.S. Department of Education, 2016).

Formative assessment. "A process used by teachers and students during instruction that provides feedback to adjust ongoing teaching and learning to improve students' achievement of intended instructional outcomes" (State Collaborative on Assessment and Student Standards, 2008, p. 3) Used to determine student readiness, monitor student progress, and inform educator of needed instructional changes.

Identification. The process of finding students who have needs for or would benefit from advanced programming or services to develop their gifts and talents. Students with gifts and talents exhibit different characteristics, traits, and ways to express their giftedness; therefore, identifying students' abilities and talents is essential to meeting their unique needs. The identification process moves from screening to placement (Matthews & Shaunessy, 2010) and involves the use of multiple measures to assess high-level ability, aptitude, achievement, or other constructs of interest in one or more areas or domains of learning (Johnsen, 2008a).

Inclusive learning environment. Inclusive learning environments are welcoming and accepting of each and every learner including those who are vulnerable to marginalization and exclusion and those who traditionally have been left out or excluded from appropriate educational and learning opportunities. Inclusion speaks to (dis)ability, race, ethnicity, culture, language, age, family status/composition, gender identity and expression, sexual orientation, socioeconomic status, religious and spiritual values, geographic location, and country of origin (Council for Exceptional Children, 2019; Council of Chief State School Officers, 2013).

Instructional strategies. Teaching and learning methods that meet the needs, interests, and abilities of students with gifts and talents. Appropriate instructional strategies would include those engaging students in inquiry, creative and critical thinking, and metacognition at a pace and level commensurate with the students' abilities. Understanding by Design (UBD), also known as 'backward design,' is often employed as an instructional strategy. UBD reflects a three-stage design process that delays the planning of classroom activities until goals have been clarified and assessments designed.

Intervention. A specific program, strategy, or set of teaching procedures used with students to help them learn.

Leadership. Ability to influence others (Reis & Housand, 2008) in a discipline (e.g., intellectual or creative leadership) or in the community (e.g., to address societal needs and problems).

Learning progressions. "Learning progressions define a coherent and continuous pathway along which students move incrementally through states of increasing competence. Every incremental state builds on and integrates the previous one as students accrue new levels of expertise with each successive step in the progression" (Renaissance Learning, 2019). Learning progressions can be used to design, differentiate, or modify instruction.

Learning progress and outcomes. Learning outcomes identify what the learner will know and be able to do by the end of a unit of study or course. Progress is assessed through an evaluation of a student's development (e.g., cognitive, psychosocial, and social and emotional growth) and tangible documentation of performance.

Lifelong learners. Individuals who seek to expand their experiences, knowledge, skills, and perspectives beyond the formal education years and continuously across the lifespan.

Local norms. Comparing students' performance on assessments with other students in their local educational setting (e.g., school or district) with the rationale that if gifted programming is aimed at identifying students who are in need of advanced instruction because they are not being challenged in their current educational setting, national comparisons are not helpful. (Plucker & Peters, 2016).

Mentorship/Internship. Connecting students with experts in a field of interest and domain of talent to work on authentic problems or tasks that allow them to authentically acquire advanced content knowledge and skills in the domain (Stephens, 2018).

Models of inquiry. An instructional model that centers learning on solving a particular problem or answering a central question. There are several different inquiry-based learning models, but most have several general elements in common: (a) learning focuses around a meaningful, well-structured problem that demands consideration of diverse perspectives (b) academic content-learning occurs as a natural part of the process as students work towards finding solutions (c) learners, working collaboratively, assume an active role in the learning process (d) teachers provide learners with learning supports and rich multiple media sources of information to assist students in successfully finding solutions, and (e) learners share and defend solutions publicly in some manner (Heik, 2019).

Ongoing assessment. An aspect of formative assessment. Regular/frequent assessments used to monitor learner progress, identify ways to help learners develop the knowledge and skills to achieve their goals, and identify any barriers to achievement (Tomlinson & Moon, 2013).

Performance-based assessment. Requires students to complete tasks or generate their own responses as a way to measure their ability to apply skills and knowledge learned from a unit of study. Sound performance-based assessments share some features with curricula for students with gifts and talents, such as focusing on open-ended questions, higher-order thinking, meta-cognitive thinking, and problem-solving. Multiple approaches in oral and written forms are preferred for assessing students' performance. Portfolios, for example, serve better as formative, rather than summative assessment (VanTassel-Baska, 2013).

Product-based assessment. Product-based assessment is considered a form of performance-based assessment (VanTassel-Baska, 2013). Different from process-oriented assessment in which skills may or may not be observable, product-based assessment evaluates the outcome of a task or assignment that is observable and measurable.

Policies and procedures. Policies and procedures translate state and federal laws, rules, and regulations into operational guidelines, protocols, and expectations of programming and services at the local level.

Professional learning plan. A professional learning plan is a working document in which an educator identifies strengths and needs for growth in relation to improving his or her practices and student outcomes.

Professional learning. Educators continuously develop their knowledge, skills, practices, and dispositions with an aim to increase their effectiveness and student outcomes (Learning Forward, 2011). Effective professional learning activities were found to have focused on teaching strategies related to specific subjects, promoted educators' active engagement in learning, created collaboration opportunities, sustained over time, and provided educators with models, coaching, and expert support (Darling-Hammond, Hyler, & Gardner, 2017).

Programming and services. Formally structured, regularly scheduled, ongoing services provided to students with gifts and talents in school or community settings (e.g., museum, laboratory, or university). Programming includes goals, student outcomes, strategies to accomplish them, and procedures for assessing and evaluating these over time, whereas services refer to educational and related interventions that may be one-time-only, annual, or ongoing, and may be provided even in the absence of formal gifted programming. Examples may include counseling, tutoring, and mentoring. Programming is understood as a comprehensive continuum of services that addresses the needs of students with gifts and talents. The Professional Standards Committee prefers the term "programming" because it indicates the ongoing nature of these services, while "program" could refer to a one-time event.

Psychosocial. The term describes "the intersection and interaction of social, cultural, and environmental influences on the mind and behavior" (American Psychological Association, n.d.). In the framework of talent development, intrinsic motivation and persistence are two basic psychosocial skills that one needs to transform abilities into creative productivity (Subotnik, 2015).

Qualitative assessment information. Assessments that use primarily words rather than numbers to describe or investigate students, teachers, parents, or other stakeholders' reactions to or perceptions of strengths or weaknesses of gifted programming and related phenomena. Interviews and portfolios (Johnsen, 2008b) are two commonly used types of qualitative instruments.

Quantitative assessment information. Numerical data (Johnsen, 2008b) used to describe performance in relation to others (e.g., norm-referenced intelligence tests) or in relation to a standard of performance (e.g., criterion-referenced achievement tests).

Resources. Human, physical, and administrative assets used to support effective teaching and learning of students with gifts and talents. Resources may include instructional personnel such as teachers, mentors, and community members as well as physical resources such as curriculum materials of any media, and facilities within and outside of the school setting. Resources also include administrative assets, such as fiscal and capital expenditures.

Self-efficacy. An individual's belief in their innate ability to achieve goals. Recent research reveals that academic and racial identity, self-efficacy, and self-esteem predict self-determined motivation and goals and have been determined to be strong predictors of academic pursuits (Byars-Winston, Diestelmann, Savoy, & Hoyt, 2017).

Self-understanding. A process of recognizing one's interests, strengths, and needs and in one's intellectual, academic, creative, leadership, and artistic abilities (domain of talent). The process results in self-knowledge with respect to one's identity, psychosocial and social-emotional development, and the influences of one's beliefs, traditions, and values on learning and behavior.

Social and emotional. Those factors from a psychological perspective that assert an affective influence on an individual's self-image, behavior, and motivation; issues such as but not limited to peer relationships, emotional adjustment, stress management, perfectionism, and sensitivity (Moon, 2003).

Social competence. The ability to interact effectively with others. Component skills include creating and maintaining positive interpersonal relationships and peer relations, asserting, and adapting oneself in social settings. Related dispositions include appreciation of human diversity, commitment to social justice, and high ethical standards (Devine, White, Ensor, & Hughes, 2016; Lee, Olszewski-Kubilius, & Thomson, 2012; Moon, 2008).

Sources of assessments. Sources of assessments include quantitative information such as standardized tests and qualitative information from teachers, administrators, counselors, families, peers, the student, and those who have information related to the student's behavior. Multiple sources of assessments provide a more comprehensive view of student behavior across different settings and different time periods (Johnsen, 2018).

Special education. In a handful of states, gifted education is included within special education (NAGC & CSDPG, 2015) and teachers of students with gifts and talents in these states are special educators. In many other locations, state law does not consider gifted education to be a part of special education and teachers of students with gifts and talents are not considered special education staff but still provide differentiated education for students.

Students with gifts and talents. This phrasing is currently preferred over "gifted and talented students" because it uses person-first language and is consistent with usage in the field of special education. The focus is on the individual's characteristics rather than the individual's label. Individuals with gifts and talents include 'gifted and talented students,' 'high ability students,' 'academically advanced students,' 'gifted students with potential' and so on.

Talent development. In gifted education, talent development involves identifying the domain-specific abilities of all students and developing the talents of those who show exceptional abilities in response to instruction and coaching (Olszewski-Kubilius, Subotnik, Worrell, & Thomson, 2018). Talent development is a long-term process in which parents, school personnel, and students work collaboratively to facilitate the development of students' talents (Feldhusen, 2001). Talent Development is also a conceptual framework for gifted education.

Technically adequate. This term refers to the psychometric properties of an assessment instrument. Instruments that are technically adequate demonstrate validity for the identified purpose, reliability in providing consistent results, minimal bias, and have been normed on a population matching the census data (Johnsen, 2008).

Twice exceptional. Also referred to as "2e," twice exceptional is the term used to describe students with gifts and talents who also give evidence of one or more disabilities as defined by federal or state eligibility criteria (e.g., specific learning disabilities (SpLD), speech and language disorders, emotional/behavioral disorders, physical disabilities, autism spectrum, etc.) (NAGC website).

Underachieving. This term refers to students who demonstrate a discrepancy between ability and performance (Reis & Housand, 2008). Underachieving students exhibit a severe discrepancy between expected achievement as measured by standardized assessments and actual achievement as measured by class grades or teacher evaluations (McCoach & Siegle, 2003). The discrepancy must persist over time and must not be the direct result of a diagnosed learning disability.

Universal screening. The tests or processes used to identify talented students are administered to an entire population (e.g., entire grade level) as opposed to only a select group of students based on an earlier screening phase or nomination procedure (Plucker & Peters, 2016).

Variety of programming. This term refers to the instructional and support options available to learners with gifts and talents, which should include a varied menu or continuum of services matching their needs. Groups as well as individual options, offered both in and outside of schools, may include but should not be limited to early entrance, grade acceleration, appropriate grouping, acceleration, enrichment, dual enrollment, online courses, curriculum compacting, apprenticeships, independent study, special classes, special schools, summer programs, and guidance and counseling services (Adams, Mursky, & Kielty, 2012).

To access the complete reference list please visit the "Programming Standards Glossary of Terms" (https://bit.ly/2019glossary) webpage.